THE ALLOYED CHURCH

The Missing link in Contemporary Christianity.

BY: kWALAH TENKU

The Missing link in Contemporary Christianity

Copyright © 2018 Kwalah Tenku

All rights reserved

This book is protected by the copyrights laws of the United States of America and should not be copied or reprinted for commercial gain or profit. The use of short quotations or occasional page copying for personal or group study is permitted and encouraged upon request. Unless otherwise identified, Scripture quotations are from the HOLY BIBLE. All emphasis within quoted scripture is the author's own.

ISBN- 13: 978-1724876676

Global Faith Coalition 6383 Deshong Dr. Lithonia GA 30058

Kwalah Tenku, Douala Cameroon

Email: kwalahtenku@gmail.com

Tel:+237) 674921131, 696185417

The Alloyed Church

INTRODUCTION

Preamble:

The church of God has for many years not fulfilled her mission as a church militant. It has distorted the essence of the church while affecting its Redemptive Integrity and its Charismatic audacity in the world - as a result of a misconception about the whole notion of 'CHURCH.'

Take the definition of CHURCH, 'as a loving family of God's people living together in fellowship.' Hence, going by this definition, the aspects of Labeling and tagging in the church will be a far-fetched and an inexistent issue, especially in Christianity. Misconceptions of the concept of CHURCH to 'edifice' and its 'ecclesiastical arrangements' have preoccupied the minds of the called to service who now look up to labels and tags as roadmaps and signs of an effective and true church of God.

Looking at contemporary Christianity and its pitfalls, there are no doubts of ecclesiastical differences, but there is an absent eschatological dimension. It is an underlying cause of all the differences leading to interdenominational conflicts and hence interfaith conflicts. It has thus led to remote and immediate cause to the prevalent apostolic deficiency in our charismatic integrity and our redemptive audacity that no more has a voice and place in our missions as a church. Hence without this eschatological dimension, labels and tags have become the modus operandi and modus Vivendi of contemporary Christianity.

The Alloyed Church

Therefore, going by the concept of CHURCH, the aspect of LOVE which acts as the 'CHURCH CPU,' have been neglected meanwhile it is the foundation and main pillar of the church. The Love for God nurtures the Love for man. The Bible attests that God is love; as you love, you are practicing and showing God first. God first in all, by this we mean no more working on our precepts but by the standard of God, leaning only on the truth of His word and relying solely on His will for our actions all through our missions. Biblical principles will, therefore, be the only and sole platform for operating our missions and will always provide a common ground for our unity as the church.

Now, one can adequately ask, 'is this what has led to a proliferation of churches with no authentic redemptive impact? 'Do Do we stand against our root foundation - Luther, who relied on the truth and sincerity of the gospel as the true basis for salvation? Has Christianity by this misplaced its rightful apostolic audacity thereby paving grounds for ongoing interfaith conflict? More so, can this be the reason for the creation of interdenominational blocks, which instead helps to split Christianity? And can this be the reason the voice of the church no more matters in handling social and state affairs? How then can the church be reconciled to take its original place without a corresponding dismantling of existing structures?

The foundation has no more been on any Biblical basis but on personal visions and particular spiritual gifts, as well as ungrounded biblical views leading to the poor spiritual base and stance that prevail. On the contrary, a theological study has been variously criticized as a great pitfall in contemporary Christianity. The bible says, 'My people die for lack of knowledge'; Is it this lack of knowledge that has resulted in what we are facing today as loopholes in ministry?

Nevertheless, Spiritual realities are most important for the effectiveness of our apostolic mandate. We must, therefore, reconcile these two things; Biblical knowledge and Gifting. Both are vital in the functioning of the Church, and its application must not be distorted to suit contextual benefits.

The church today is that which loves God but not the realities of God. It is rather so unfortunate that there is a considerable discrepancy between the love for God and obeying the realities of God. It initially is not the intended Church of God. The Church of God has to be that of obeying of spiritual realities resulting in ensuing impacts seen in the life of the church with rippling effects on society. Instead, the church has been the platform for personal views on scriptural and spiritual realities vis a vis personal egoistic tendencies. This discredits the Biblical vision of 'Unity of the Spirit in the bond of peace' (Ephesians 4:3). Worst of all is the aspect of the 'Jesus Junior Syndrome' which has invaded contemporary Christianity, leading the church and the essence of the gospel at the back seat of church life. Spiritual gimmicks have become the measuring rod of the authenticity of contemporary Christianity, giving the church a more carnal orientation than the spiritual impetus deserved.

'Insofar as there is jealousy, strife, and factions among you, aren't you fleshly, and don't you walk in the ways of men? For when one says, "I follow Paul," and another, "I follow Apollos," aren't you fleshly? Who then is Apollos, and who is Paul, but servants through whom you

*believed; and each as the Lord gave to him? I planted. Apollos watered. But God gave the increase. So then neither he who plants is anything, nor he who waters, but God who gives the increase.'***(1 Cor. 3:3-7)**

It is rather a paradox with contemporary Christianity that, knowing the church is much more than knowing our God (Jesus) who is head of the church. If the church were to go by what God told Daniel; 'Those who know their God shall be strong and do exploits' (Daniel 11:32), then all the gimmicks and struggles for signs and wonders will be an inexistent thing in the church. Here we find the essence of the Great Commission being questionable in the life of today's Church and the whole leadership concept in the church misinterpreted.

The church today tries only to understand and manifest Spiritual Gifts but ignore the Giver of the Gifts. It has determined the kind of fights we have in the church today. The church does more of physical fighting while ignoring the Internal Fights, which are more spiritually benefitting. It has led to a perpetually laborious and an unproductive Christian Church.

For we wrestle not against flesh and blood, but against principalities, against powers, against the rulers of the darkness of this world, against spiritual wickedness in high places. **(Eph 6:12)**

The Internal success is more impactful to both the physical and Spiritual life of the Christians and the Church; the efficacy of

Matt 6:33 *'But seek ye first the kingdom of God, and his righteousness, and all these things shall be added unto you.'*

There is cool church war in almost all the churches you see around you - where they are all the Christian virtues we see in the scripture:
Pursue righteousness, faith, love, and peace with those who call on the Lord out of a pure heart.
2 Tim. 2:22

Reproach has been the order of the church today as the apostolic mandate of the Church has been rendered overt to doubts; all because its prophetic audacity has lost its original impetus. This has now led the church instead of trying to defend its stance and ignore what God told Joshua, *'be strong'* and NOT *'act strong.'*

'Yet now be strong, O Zerubbabel, saith the LORD; and be strong, O Joshua, son of Josedech, the high priest; and be strong, all ye people of the land.' **(Hag 2:4)**

The church is now simply acting strong rather than being strong through the imbibing of all its spiritual Impetus in the life of the Church.

Today, mental dexterity has taken the place of Spiritual Awesomeness. This has made the essence of the gospel to lost its impetus as the basis of our Christian and church modus operandi and Modus Vivendi. Artifice 'exegesis' has become the order of the today's church to achieve its selfish motives. This has rendered the church volatile to the critics of even unbelievers; who now see the church with an ordinary eye and hence doubt and combat its apostolic mandate.

Most of all, Christians and the Church are signposts. Somewhat, signposts such as; humility, leadership, and quality assurance have all been ignored. These signposts stand as a manual for all our operations as a church. In as much as they are violated, the move to achieve effective results becomes a far-fetched dream because the pathway to mount the spiritual steps has been neglected. By this, we keep on witnessing a constant 'Spiritual Recession' resulting in common results achieved in the lives of the Christians.

It is worthy of note that love in the church should and will be essentially seen from the points of; giving, prayers, communication, relationship, faith, obedience, knowledge and the true nature of Christ in you towards each other and to God.

We will be exploring these facets and more to make an appraisal, making a retrospect and introspection on how the church can regain its Prophetic audacity and charismatic integrity as the church of God owing in mind that we are co-laborers in His vineyard. For until the church restructures its functioning in line with scriptural and spiritual norms, the whole essence of the church will remain questionable.

Until we all attain to the unity of the faith, and of the knowledge of the Son of God, to mature manhood, of the measure of the stature of the fullness of Christ. **Eph 4:13**

I would like us to use the biblical chemistry approach to study the scriptural text above. "Biblical chemistry is an analytic, systematic, and Investigative study of the worth in biblical words and phrases and the sense ingrained in biblical sentences." When I look at our above text with the eyes of a Biblical Chemist, I see an obligation in the hands of the denominationalist in the aspect of the unity of faith, based on the knowledge of Christ Jesus that can make us seamless on to the image Christ. I thank God for the course biblical chemistry for it methodology that has to reawaken a scripture that was given to me in a vision in 2013. In the vision, I saw all churches coming together in a single hall to discourse on the unity of faith in the body of Christ. Biblical chemistry has helped to enlighten the eyes of my understanding to see this vision clearer. We will be carrying out a biblical chemistry analysis of **Eph 4:13**, considering the word constituent as they relate to our subject.

Each time God has a plan for the world, He makes sure that it is revealed through his servant to his people so that they can rightly execute it according to His will. The scripture says that; *God made us perfect in every good work to do his will working in us through Christ.*

'Make you perfect in every good work to do his will, working in you that which is well pleasing in his sight, through Jesus Christ; to whom be glory forever and ever. Amen.'

(Heb 13:21)

PREFACE

The appearance of this book looks so nominal but in actual terms it's a broad scope fundamental resource to reawaken our sense and duty of the church as the body of Christ as rightly instituted by Jesus. This material can add an inch of sense and reminder to a people throughout the world who are engaged on the frontiers of the Church's Mission. The body of Christ coordinates all other Theological tasks of transforming the world through the transformative power of the gospel of Christ.

I confess that I have drawn freely from the works of many authors, not with the aim of claiming credit for the wisdom of others, but rather to make their wisdom access spheres that would render the material in another purposeful essence to the Church.

History portrays that the Church always declines in numbers, impact and vitality when it becomes preoccupied with itself. Contemporary Christianity is exposed to a proliferation of paradigms and models leading to such legalistic religious structures that now outstretch all over to represent the Church. Paul's Church planting ministry despite others odds always determined to keep the purpose of the Church as, 'the true Church of Christ' with a series of Biblical Checklist used by Paul to guide them.

More so, the decline in piety and a laxity of moral and Spiritual audacity has plagued the Church which is now deteriorating to a mere human structure with nominal norms yet an

Eschatological expectancy. The Alloyed Church therefore will never give an apt respond to the Church's eschatological needs.

Using a strong scriptural basis to this book, we see Paul who more than any other New Testament leader and author, outlines and explains God's manifesto for the Church both at personal level and most of all as a Corporate body. Dissecting the portion into fragments portrays an insightful counsel regarding the discernment of true experiences of revival that must be re-enacted in the Church to reinstate its original audacity and purpose as an institution of the God's Kingdom 'Ecclesia' of fellowship with His people.

An 'Itinerant Church' is what awaits the future of the Church which initially is intended to tarry till the second coming of Jesus who is as scripture enjoins is to come and meet 'a Church without blemish.'

My personal prayer is that this study will help you – Professional Pastor or Lay person – to look first at your own Spiritual walk and then as a corporate body, so as to determine the extent to which we measure up to "the measure of the Stature of the fullness of Christ." Most of all, may it be able to lead to a Church that reflects Christ's life in their walk together as a Corporate body of Christ, as instituted by the architect of the Church, Christ Himself.

TABLE OF CONTENTS

INTRODUCTION 3

PREFACE 10

1) Until we all attain 13

2) To the Unity 19

3) Of the faith 26

4) And knowledge 33

5) Of the Son of God 37

6) Unto a perfect man 41

7) A measure of the stature 46

8) The fullness of Christ 50

BIBLIOGRAPHY 52

The Missing link in Contemporary Christianity

CHAPTER ONE

UNTIL WE ALL ATTAIN

« There is a vacuum in the body of Christ that needs to be fulfilled «

Until we all attain to the unity of the faith, and of the knowledge of the Son of God, to mature manhood, of the measure of the stature of the fullness of Christ.
EPH 4:13

Until we all attain: It means that we still have a lot to do both physically and spiritually. There is a vacuum in the body of Christ that needs to be fulfilled.'Until' in the above scripture communicates a sense of obligation and expectation. "Until" connotes continuity, which means there is a process and every process has steps required for attainment.

'So God created man in his image, in the image of God created he him; male and female created He them. And God blessed them, and God said unto them, Be fruitful, and multiply, and replenish the earth, and subdue it: and have dominion over the fish of the sea, and over the fowl of the air, and over every living thing that moveth upon the earth So God created man in his image, in the image of God created he him; male and female created He them. And God blessed them, and God said unto them, Be fruitful, and multiply, and replenish the earth, and subdue it: and have dominion over the fish of the sea, and over the fowl of the air, and over every living thing that moveth upon the earth.'
(Gen 1:27-28.)

After God had finished with creation, He created man in his image, and the above scripture shows the kind of competence God bestowed in humankind to be fruitful, multiply, and replenish the earth, subdue and have dominion over everything.

God rested on the seventh day because He gave the man (male and female) all it takes to continue from where he ended. Look at what the scripture says in the book of Job.

'Thou shall also decree a thing, and it shall be established unto thee: and the light shall shine upon thy ways.'
(Job 22:28)

If there is anything wrong in the body of Christ and we choose to be silent that makes us accomplices to the error. The reason is that we have been given the mandate on the earth realm to change things and to bring all things into harmony with the truth. Creation awaits us to act and decree things and bring them to pass. In the beginning, God limited man's authority just to earth, but today we can create in the universe through Jesus Christ.

The bible says; *'For the earnest expectation of the creature waiteth for the manifestation of the sons of God. For the creature was made subject to vanity, not willingly, but because of him who hath subjected the same in hope, Because the creature itself also shall be delivered from the bondage of corruption into the glorious liberty of the children of God.For we know that the whole creation groaneth and travaileth in pain together until now.'*
(Rom 8:19-22)

Until we all attain:
'We' connotes collectivity: What we are called to do is a collective task, which makes the unity of the body of Christ a dire need.

The bible says;

'And he gave some, apostles; and some, prophets; and some, evangelists; and some, pastors and teachers; for the perfecting of the saints, for the work of the ministry, for the edifying of the body of Christ'
(Eph 4:11-12)

So, the lone ranger mentality within the body of Christ is creating division and disunity in the body of Christ, hampering collectiveness in diversity. The above situation has led to the individualistic concept of building empires around the world in the name of ministry for selfish interests forgetting the essence of Christianity. Jesus Christ, our Lord, promoted togetherness.

'For where two or three are gathered together in my name, there am I in the midst of them.' **(Matt 18:20)**

In the very depth of the mind of God is the idea for humankind to work collectively. During creation, we see how God said, *"let us [father, son, and Holy Spirit] create man in our own image and likeness'* - **Gen 1:26.AMP BIBLE**

Apostle Paul spoke here with much confidence as concerning attending the aspiration of every called minister of God in the Christian race.

Until we all attain:

'ALL' connotes the representation of everyone in the body of Christ in union with the Holy Spirit. The church cannot effectually exist without the power of the Holy Spirit who is the empowerment and guide of the church.

'But ye shall receive power, after that, the Holy Ghost comes upon you: and ye shall be witnesses unto me both in Jerusalem, and in all Judaea, and in Samaria, and unto the uttermost part of the earth.' (**Act 1:8**)

So, if we were to go by the definition of the CHURCH as a happy family of Gods people living together in fellowship in the knowledge of Christ - fellowship both with "man" and the Godhead must merge to form the life of the Church. This makes the Church have a spiritual identity uncommon to any other gathering.

Until we all attain:
'ATTAIN' signifies a breakthrough that needs to be achieved, a vacuum that needs to be filled, bridging the gap for the unity required in the body of Christ. It indicates that the church still has a task to fulfill the command of the great commission and to continue with the Pentecost revival.

'And all things are of God, who hath reconciled us to himself by Jesus Christ, and hath given to us the ministry of reconciliation; To wit, that God was in Christ, reconciling the world unto himself, not imputing their trespasses unto them; and hath committed unto us the word of reconciliation.'
(2Cor 5:18-19).

The above scriptural text stresses on the word reconciliation, which is the mission of the great commission, reconciling the world to Christ is the task every born Christian must fulfill in life. If we have received the ministry of reconciliation (unifying) the world to Christ, then the question here is; 'How can you reconcile in the division?'

The body of Christ until now has not yet set the right machinery for its functioning. The unity of the body of Christ is the only tool to attain the redemptive purpose of the church. Unity characterized the life of Jesus and His disciples as well as the early church not in buildings but the message. After the death and resurrection of Christ, the church was given the mandate to carry on with the unifying mission of Jesus - to bring the redemptive message intended for the world. Therefore the oneness of the body of Christ stands as the only useful tool to attain the redemptive purpose for humankind.
'A new commandment I give unto you, that ye love one another; as I have loved you, that ye also love one another. By this shall all men know that ye are my disciples if ye have love one to another'.
(John 13:34-35.)

Take note of the words to love one another as the most convincing evidence of Christian living. The tenacity of the church to carry on its task up till fulfillment is the only "CPU" to attend its mission and purpose to the world while recognizing and maintaining the place of the Godhead.

The Missing link in Contemporary Christianity

CHAPTER TWO

TO THE UNITY

«The church has in her prophecy a future of perfect unity»

The Alloyed Church

In one of his sermon, renowned London preacher, *C. H. Spurgeon* declared;

"Everywhere, in all sects, I see inventions of men arrogating the place of the commandments of God. Let us sweep our temples, and return unto the word of the Lord. Say not that ye believe the Book when you act as though it were not true – Will they believe it? Will they practice it? Will they abide by the standard?" – From the sermon: Nominal Christians – Real Infidels.

The above words are relevant even to today's church that has neglected and seemingly acts contrary to the tenets of the Christian mission. In all ramifications, the essence and purpose of the mission of the church have been distorted and almost misinterpreted in our service as the church towards the fulfillment of the gospel of salvation and the kingdom of God.

The whole essence of the gospel is that; *there should be no Schism in the body of Christ – Unity.*

Unity can be seen from the point of its definition to mean a state of being in full agreement: oneness, without deviation or change of the totality of related parts: an entity that is complex or systematic whole. Going by this definition, the aspect of unity is seen as a continuous process with a focal point of agreement, oneness, continuity, no change in a complex related system.

This is the unity system to be found in the Church. The church has in her prophecy a future of perfect unity, but that shouldn't be an excuse for not working in it now. The Bible tells us that we are, 'All one in Christ' but this unity must be demonstrated in practical ways with fellowship and love as central elements.

The church is His. It is made up of the Redeemed. Jesus purchased the church with His blood.

'Take heed therefore unto yourselves, and to all the flock, over the which the Holy Ghost hath made you overseers, to feed the church of God, which he hath purchased with his blood.'
(Acts 20:28)

Additionally, the Church of Jesus the Christ also stands firmly established in the love and purpose of God. The Church is the body of Christ, and He is head over all things to it, and He is Savior of it. Since the church is the body of Christ, we should realize how important it is to keep that body pure. So, the problem comes when the church is blemished and spotted with sin; causing a deviation from what God authorized.

The pivotal role of the Church can be seen as; Through the church, the manifold wisdom of God is made known to the world. It is in the church: the body of the redeemed over which Christ is head, that God and His purpose are glorified. The love of Christ and the death of Christ are revealed as being for the Church, It is the body to which all the saved-the reconciled are added, and the Church is one body.

Regrettably far too many do not have a biblical view of the church. When our view is not biblical, we are short-changed. Seeing the Church in its biblical simplicity and beauty then we need to understand that it is in the church that believers have communion with God and fellowship with one another. The

Lord's Church as revealed in the Bible is a perfect organization, and it reveals the perfect plan of salvation.

Unfortunately, the contrary 'Indifference' is the most difficult of all problems in the church to deal with as many in the church are not against what we are trying to do nor are they really for it making the church untrustworthy. Meanwhile, before spreading the gospel, the church must prepare for the sowing by earning the right to be heard – untrustworthiness steals this right.

'I know thy works, that thou art neither cold nor hot: I would thou wert cold or hot. So then because of thou art lukewarm, and neither cold nor hot, I will spue thee out of my mouth.'
(Revelations 3:15-16)

We are witnessing in the church today one of the saddest losses of the prophetic and apostolic vision. Many preachers are compromising and sacrificing truth to ingratiate themselves with the misled groups. This proffered fellowship with those in error hinders others who are striving to lead the church to its purpose and essence.

The main goal of the Christian Mission is being neglected. The Church despite its differences in doctrines and ecclesiastical arrangements, there is only One Mission as was Jesus' – *"The son of man is come to seek and to save the lost."*

[Luke 19: 10]

Jesus passed that mission unto His disciples and now unto us, as He said in a prayer to the Father, *"As thou sent me into the world, so I have sent them into the world"* – One Mission.

Most importantly looking at the root criteria for our mission – being a Christian, it is best to know who is a Christian. *A Christian is, 'one who has a mind and knows it. He has a will and shows it. He sees the way and goes it. He draws the line and toes it. He has a chance and takes it. A friendly hand and shakes it. A rule- He never breaks it. If there's no time, he makes it. He loves the truth and Stands by it. Never, ever would deny it. He hears a lie and slays it. He owes a debt and pays it. He sees the path Christ trod, and grips the hand of God, and follows it'.* Going by this definition, the elements therein should form the rudiments of our practice in Mission.

The 'Elijah question,' *"Ask what I shall do for you before I am taken from you"* should be our Passion Booster, Mission Motivator, Mission Obligation and Mission Responsibility for the Church. Elijah though in the Old Testament times, was also involved in the Mission of God which he was to hand over to Elisha to continue the task. This is unlike today where the *Christian mission has become an affair of a 'Dynasty of families'*-only particular people concentrate on themselves and their service with no thought of passing on to the younger generations. The Church must deal with change effectively. We must learn to change some things, but always to maintain our focus on the unchanging priorities and goals of God and of the Church.

Now, revisiting the Priesthood of the Church, our High Priest today is Jesus Christ, the son of God. Under Him all other priesthood and laity in the Church function as Sub-priests. This helps to wipe away the 'Jesus Junior Syndrome' in Church today. His model of ministry should be the modus operandi in ministry and mission. Many ministerial pitfalls have set in for lack of tutorship from the Priesthood mentor, Jesus. Instead, gimmicks have become the order of the day to showcase a prophetic authentication of our mission.

The *Redemptive Voice, Purpose, and Mission of the Church* has been derailed and misplaced. Everything in the Church must be recognized as authorized by God. He has designed a perfect plan of salvation for the Church. So the Church's perfection is retained by the way it deals with imperfection- the human element in the church is as imperfect as its members. But the Church has a perfect Savior who holds before us His perfect life for our goal, saying, 'Follow Me' **[Mathew 16:24]** This should be the voice, purpose, and mission of the Church. For the Church offers strength to help us in our weaknesses, courage when we are fainthearted, comfort when we are sad, and "joy unspeakable and full of glory" **[1 Peter 1:3]**. When all these are absent, the Church's Redemptive audacity will become obsolete, and her mission defeated.

Relating to contemporary Christianity which intends to claim a new turn around in Christianity, the essence of true biblical Christianity based upon the freedom in Christ could still be propagated, yet in a new and credible form. Jesus Christ Himself who constitutes the spiritual power of scripture should be revealed to the people. In this way, the unity of the church will be achieved – Church celestial and Church Militant.

Worthy of note is the aspect of the exercise and study of theology today. Jesus Christ is the source and measure of Faith and Theology in the church: 'Norma Normans non normal' This mindset conditions the doctrines and functioning of the church towards the purpose of the kingdom. Theology in the Church should, therefore, base on – Hierarchy of Truths and Scripture Centered.

Most of all, the two pillars of Unity in the Church must be upheld – Unity of Faith and Unity of the Spirit. We must hold the truth in love and urge it with grace, but never allow it to sever the bond, of peace which unites us to all who are allowed by God's Spirit. This forms the common ground for the church to adjust its strides in kingdom walk; could be in a Denominational yet Spiritual Synergy.

CHAPTER THREE

OF THE FAITH

"The true transforming power of the Church is God Himself."

Considering the basic rule; *there can be only one true Church - the body of Christ. It is made up of real Christians - of all who believe in Christ and His gospel. Every man and woman who:*

"Believes that Jesus Christ is God's son,

Conceived of the Holy Spirit,

Born of a virgin, who came as God in the flesh.

Who bore our sins for us in His death on the Cross

Who shed His blood for the remission of our sins.

Who died for us and was raised from the dead for our justification,

Who is now forever seated at the right of God?

And makes intercessions for our sins' (Mathew 16:24-27, John 1:43, John 12:26, John 21:19-22

Then the disillusionment in today century church can never be transformed since the basic fundamental fact of Christianity is kept in the background.

The true transforming power of the Church is God Himself. Scripture and history tell us that miracles tend to happen more frequently when there is a revival, and God is pouring out His grace on a city.

There are two aspects; the receiving of Faith and the Acting out of God's will in faith – are to be the single operating wheel of the Christian Church.

The basic relationship with God is by faith and not any medication. Faith in Bible days was not established –no land, no Torah, no Temple. Such was the Abrahamic Faith which operated quite well without any guiding institutions and still produced a man as great as Moses.

Rather we have turned Christianity into another *"Seven Steps to personal success":* focusing on ourselves and neglecting the eternal – no genuine Faith, no Sacrifice, no zeal.

The gospel proclaimed truthfully is not 'marketable' or commercially acceptable **(2nd Cor.4:17)**; it offends many with the offense of the cross and arouses deep hostility and persecution.

Most of all, the greatest focal point of Christianity – Salvation, requires just two things: Repentance and Faith.

Worthy of note is the fact that new Christians have become confused by the different denominational doctrines and the blackmail of each other; lauding their doctrinal virtuosity and seeking to proselyte members from each other.

The Christian Faith is simply keeping eyes on Jesus Christ and on what He said and taught, following Him as the only way. Following Christ implies to love, serve, worship, learn and to fellowship with Him in prayers, His word and obeying all therein – cardinal fundamentals of the Gospel.

Most profoundly, Jesus made a statement about the founding of His CHURCH; The true Church is established upon the revelation of faith that Jesus Christ is the son of God. That revelation is and should be not only the foundation but the modus operandi of the Christian Church and its modus Vivendi. The cardinal facts of the Gospel, therefore, become the prerequisite for actively being part of the CHURCH.

Emphasis should be made as to the Cardinal facts of the ONE TRUE CHURCH –the Body of Christ; Jesus Christ Himself founded it, Jesus is the Corner Stone, and Jesus is the foundation, *"No other foundation can be laid than that which is laid by Jesus Christ."* Christ is the founder, the builder, and the Church belongs to Him alone.

The Apostle Paul said the essence of the true church is *"CHRIST IN YOU, the hope of glory."* You may "JOIN" and fellowship with a community of believers in any assembly, but your REAL MEMBERSHIP, your new SPIRITUAL BIRTH, and BIRTHRIGHT is registered in the Lamb's Book of Life in Heaven.

Then, the underlying basic beliefs and doctrines of all Christian denominations are fundamentally the same:

Jesus Christ was conceived of the Holy Spirit.

He was born of a virgin

He was God in the flesh, "Emmanuel…God with us."

His blood was Divine

His life showed us the will of God.

He died to pay our debts, bearing our sins.

He rose again for our justification.

He lives today seated at God's right hand to ever make intercession for us as the only Mediator between God and us.

He is man's only Saviour.

(Mathew 1:23, John 6:38, John 14:6, John 5:24, John 8:12, Ephesians 4:13-16)

The Church has so much been characterized by failing to move with God both individually and corporately. Worst is even the reluctance on the part of the leaders (Ministers) to allow the sword(Spirit of Truth) to cut through freely, fully and forever especially from the legalism of Christianity. The cause has been stemmed from resistance to accepting Change. The Church must be seen from and operate on the Reality of the Church being Colonies of Heaven; miniatures of 'The Jerusalem that is above' and hence providing on earth a corporate expression of 'the glorious freedom of the Children of God.'

Worthy of note is that the Christian Church must realise that the CHURCH is the body of Christ and so operates under a Covenant of Faith. This Covenant acts as the determinant and prerequisite to fully engaging the fullness therein the life, joy, and privileges involved in Kingdom Ministration.

Therefore, paradigm shifts of the Christian Faith propelled by various established doctrines, and denominational influences have disrupted the real essence and purpose of the existence of the church. The foundations, Initial rules, and Principles of the Christian Faith must be re-enacted before the oneness, and the Unity of the Body of Christ can be evident.

In all, the whole misconception of the Christian Faith and its Tenets has created a whole handicap in personal Christian faith leading to the alloyed church of today. So till we come to the stage of avoiding such admixture of Christian Personal Views, then can we come to the Faith that coordinates and propels our Christian Charisma.

On the other hand, there is a necessary level of this admixture with the Divine that must be enacted as a basis for Christian Operations. Jesus talking to Peter enjoins the acknowledgment of His divine Supreme Audacity as the basis and foundation of the CHURCH. Again to the disciples, Jesus re-enacts the Divine Mandate over the Church to the Mentorship of the Holy Spirit. Until this admixture with the Divine is re-enacted and concerning the power of the Divine, the Apostolic Audacity and Charismatic Integrity of the Body of Christ cannot showcase.

The Faith of the Church is the Focal Point of Christian life and Christianity as a whole. Therefore till we attain this basis of our

Christian strides, then the Church will not attain and experience the full level of Unity that ought to be in the Christian church.

The Missing link in Contemporary Christianity

CHAPTER FOUR

OF THE KNOWLEDGE

"This is the knowledge required for the church to comprehend the true power of God fully."

The Alloyed Church

The church of Jesus Christ is already delving into a dispensation in which believers will not more relate with God base on denomination and power demonstration but by the knowledge of Christ Jesus. The knowledge of God is now spreading everywhere that only the love of the truth can help us recognize it.

'For the earth, shall be filled with the knowledge of the glory of the LORD, as the waters cover the sea.' **(Hab 2:14)**

Knowledge is defined as the information, understanding or skill that is acquired through education or experience, the state is aware of something.

The knowledge the scripture is talking about is the knowledge of God; which is divine truth, personified in Christ. When we receive it, we will be transformed into living epistles of the knowledge of God. It is in Christ that the fullness of the Godhead dwells. As our lead scripture mentions, it makes you a perfect man and brings you to the stature of the fullness of Christ.

From a biblical perspective, knowledge is not from obsolete points of view, but from a spiritual perspective as an endowment. Therefore Knowledge is essential in the understanding and execution of any ministerial area of calling. Peter and John after receiving the Holy Ghost acted not of their own will but the knowledge of God and exhibited the message of salvation rightly as in the scripture below.

'Neither is there salvation in any other: for there is none another name under heaven given among men, whereby we must be saved. Now when they saw the boldness of Peter and John and perceived that they were unlearned and ignorant men, they marveled; and they took

knowledge of them, that they had been with Jesus. And beholding the man which was healed standing with them, they could say nothing against it. But when they had commanded them to go aside out of the council, they conferred among themselves.' **(Acts 4:12-15)**

The Pentecost experience marks the turning point of the church through the empowerment of the Holy Spirit who pivots the church and acts as the machinery for its operation. Empowering the church, Holy Spirit has embedded the church with gifts with one of it being - Word of Knowledge; that the church might experience the revelatory power of the grace of God.

'And hath put all things under his feet, and gave him to be the head over all things to the church, which is his body, the fullness of him that filleth all in all.' **(Eph 1:22-23.)**

One of such gifts as recorded in **1 Corinthians 12:8** is the word of knowledge by the spirit of God. This is the knowledge required for the church to comprehend the true power of God fully.
'For to one is given by the Spirit the word of wisdom; to another the word of knowledge by the same Spirit.'

Such Knowledge helps the believer to know God and his will - build the zeal, passion, and understanding with the great revelation of the prophetic in the word of God. Lack of this divine knowledge makes the church to depend on its doctrinal voice than the true basis of the Christian faith which is the word of God, our faith builder.

'So then faith cometh by hearing and hearing by the word of God. **(Rom 10:17.)**

The Alloyed Church

The knowledge of God is the word of God, and the word of God is Jesus Christ. When you accept Christ as your Lord and savior, you are indeed saved, but that alone doesn't give you the capacity to access the mind of God that has been revealed to this generation.

'But God hath revealed them unto us by his Spirit: for the Spirit searcheth all things, yea, the deep things of God. For what man knoweth the things of a man, save the spirit of man which is in him? Even so, the things of God knoweth no man, but the Spirit of God. Now we have received, not the spirit of the world, but the spirit which is of God; that we might know the things that are freely given to us of God. Which things also we speak, not in the words which man's wisdom teacheth, but which the Holy Ghost teacheth; comparing spiritual things with spiritual. But the natural man receiveth, not the things of the Spirit of God: for they are foolishness unto him: neither can he know them, because they are spiritually discerned. But he that is spiritual judgeth all things, yet he is judged of no man. For who hath known the mind of the Lord, that he may instruct him? But we have the mind of Christ.' **(1Cor 2:11-16)**

The knowledge of God makes you grow spiritually as a Christian having a better understanding of the unity of the faith which is the central point of the existence of the church. Check the text below.

'Yes truly, and I am ready to give up all things for the knowledge of Christ Jesus my Lord, which is more than all: for whom I have undergone the loss of all things, and to me, they are less than nothing, so that I may have Christ as my reward.' **(Philippians 3:8)**

CHAPTER FIVE

OF THE SON OF GOD

« He took away our iniquities and made provision for salvation in all aspects and sphere of life »

Son takes charge, while children wait for Order.
In the days of old, each time they used the word son, it referred to an heir, that is to say someone who is capable of succeeding the father in power, authority, sound judgment and can accommodate others, to take charge and has the capacity to execute function not only after the death of their father but even when they are still alive. A son is he who is after the father or whom the father has willed all to him. The text below, Jesus shows the relationship between father and son, with having the full right to implement the decision.

'All things are delivered to me of my Father: and no man knoweth who the Son is, but the Father; and who the Father is, but the Son, and he to whom the Son will reveal him.'
   (Luk 10:22.)

In the Old Testament, faith was the basis of a relationship with God. God is omnipresent and manifested his presence in various forms, and Isaiah described Him as in the scripture below

'In their affliction, he was afflicted, and the angel of his presence saved them: in his love and his pity he redeemed them, and he bares them, and carried them all the days of old. But they rebelled, and vexed his holy Spirit: therefore he was turned to be their enemy, and he fought against them.'
   (Isa 63:9-10)

From the fall of man, God has always wanted a spotless and new relationship with His people. As a result, God sent his only son and heir to his throne in human form, who came as a true representative of the person of God; manifested in human and spirit form. Jesus Christ came as the true and visible representation of the word of God in which all things are found, to emphasize the Old Testament belief and the power of God which basis is by faith.

'Giving thanks unto the Father, which hath made us meet to be partakers of the inheritance of the saints in light: Who hath delivered us from the power of darkness, and hath translated us into the kingdom of his dear Son: In whom we have redemption through his blood, even the forgiveness of sins: Who is the image of the invisible God, the firstborn of every creature: For by him were all things created, that are in heaven, and that are in earth, visible and invisible, whether they be thrones, or dominions, or principalities, or powers: he created all things, and for him: And he is before all things and by him all things consist.'
(Col 1:13-17)

As our lead scripture emphasizes the knowledge of the Son of God; knowing the son means knowing the Father. Nevertheless, scripture emphasizes the person of Jesus Christ as the only son of God; the church needs to understand the Person, Message, Mission and Role of Jesus Christ in his body.

During the time of Jesus, the faith, knowledge and worshiping of God were centered in Jerusalem with the teachers of the law who took the Jewish believers captive. Jesus therefore with the capacity of a son, confronted them and spoke of himself as the giver of knowledge and eternal life of God viral amongst the Jews.

To fulfill his mission as a son of his father; Jesus Christ enabled this power to move to Samaria and to the other nations of the world with the Holy Spirit on a guardian assignment to ensure the divine purpose of the church accomplished. Most importantly the son of God has been made a sacrifice for humankind to deliver us from the power of the law that kept man distant from the glory of God.

As the son of God, Jesus proved his authority over all things by his death and resurrection. He took away our iniquities and made provision for salvation in all aspects and sphere of life. Thus, knowing the son of God gives us all that pertains to life and godliness.

'Grace and peace be multiplied unto you through the knowledge of God, and of Jesus, our Lord, According as his divine power hath given unto us all things that pertain unto life and godliness...'
(2Peter 1:2-4)

Think about this, as a son Jesus reconciled us to his father and made us co-heirs with him. Now you are a son, what are the responsibilities that you have taken that bring others in the kingdom of your Father. Wake-up!

CHAPTER SIX

UNTO A PERFECT MAN

« You become transformed in your manner of thinking »

'When I was a child, I spoke as a child, I understood as a child, I thought as a child: but when I became a man, I put away childish things.'
(1Co 13:11)

"Perfect man" perfection in other word means without blame, being pure, or being sinless. But in this contest perfect man means to be mature or to be filled with the knowledge of Christ which is Christ. Maturity is the ability to reveal Christ through our lives and the knowledge of the word. This brings us to a place of the knowledge of Christ Jesus and the principal mission of God for creation. The text below admonished us to continue in the study of the word.

'But continue thou in the things which thou hast learned and hast been assured of, knowing of whom thou hast learned them; And that from a child thou hast known the holy scriptures, which can make thee wise unto salvation through faith which is in Christ Jesus.'
(2Ti 3:14-15)

A perfect man is one who is in Jesus Christ and Christ in him. When Christ is in you and you in him, you will become a brand new person different from the person you were before meeting Christ. God changes you and gives you the desire to be guided by the principles of Christ, which are in your new nature. You become transformed in your manner of thinking, living and doing things. You develop in the mind of Christ in you. Maturity in Christ also signifies that you are qualified to represent him as an ambassador in this world. An Ambassador is one who represents a nation in another nation. As a perfect man, you will become a corporate- archetype of Christ here on earth. If we are perfect, it will show in righteous and most especially, we will be carriers of the accurate knowledge of God.

With these, you have the capacity and authority to act like Christ in this world.

> 'The first man is of the earth, earthy: the second man is the Lord from heaven. As is earthy, such are they also that are earthy: and as is heavenly, such are they also that are heavenly. And as we have borne the image of the earthy, we shall also bear the image of the heavenly.'

(1Co 15:47-49)

Perfection is attained only in Christ Jesus; every perfect fellow is seen in their life which is emulating Christ teachings and lifestyle, love, fellowship, and harmony. Scriptures make us understand that perfection is attainable through the studying of the word of God.

> 'Whereby, when ye read, ye may understand my knowledge in the mystery of Christ) Which in other ages was not made known unto the sons of men, as it is now revealed unto his holy apostles and prophets by the Spirit.'

(Eph 3:4-5)

> 'But continue thou in the things which thou hast learned and hast been assured of, knowing of whom thou hast learned them; And that from a child thou hast known the holy scriptures, which can make thee wise unto salvation through faith which is in Christ Jesus. All scripture is given by inspiration of God, and is profitable for doctrine, for reproof, for correction, for instruction in righteousness: That the man of God may be perfect, thoroughly furnished unto all good works.'

(2Ti 3:14 -17)

Perfection is a nature of God which makes us complete as Christians in His the fullness. It makes us one with God by giving us the access to operating as God in this dispensation of the revelation of Christ. In essence, it makes us ready candidates for the heavenly crown that awaits making us reconciliation ministers and demonstrators of the power of the gospel of Christ. Every perfect man is a mature minister of the good news of Jesus Christ with a special mandate of reconciling the world back to God by the power of the Holy Ghost.

The characteristics of a mature man in Christ is seen in the fruits you produce through the following aspects:

1. Preaching the gospel.

2. The main aim of winning a soul for the kingdom of God.

3. Perfection is seen in love,

'I in them, and thou in me, that they may be made perfect in one; and that the world may know that thou hast sent me, and hast loved them, as thou hast loved me.'

(John 17:23)

Perfection is one of the most important aspects of Christianity, without it we cannot face God or obtain solutions.

'But we see Jesus, who was made a little lower than the angels for the suffering of death, crowned with glory and honor; that he by the grace of God should taste death for every man. For it became him, for who are all things, and by whom are all things, in bringing many sons unto glory, to make the captain of their salvation perfect through sufferings. For both he that sanctifieth and they who are sanctified are all of one: for which cause he is not ashamed to call them brethren.'
(Heb 2:10-11)

Perfection brings us, a place of love and a sound mind;

'For God hath not given us the spirit of fear; but of power, and of love, and of a sound mind.'

(2 Timothy 1:7)

CHAPTER SEVEN

MEASURE OF THE STATURE

« Here we are talking about the measure in Christ which is the access to the status of Christ »

Let's take note of the words Measure and Stature

The measure means to attain dimension; state fits for a task that already exists or presuming. Attaining a task does not depend on the height or size of an individual, but on the how you understand the concept of the task laid before you.

'When I was a child, I spake as a child, I understood as a child, I thought as a child: but when I became a man, I put away childish things.' **(1Co 13:11)**

'Now I say, That the heir, as long as he is a child, differeth nothing from a servant, though he is lord of all., **(Gal 4:1)**

'That we henceforth are no more children, tossed to and fro, and carried about with every wind of doctrine, by the sleight of men, and cunning craftiness, whereby they lie in wait to deceive.' **(Eph4:14)**

From the above scriptures, it is evident that there is a measure of understanding that makes you fit for a task. Biblically your measure determines your quality, influence, and impact in your world. Here we are talking about the measure in Christ which is the access to the status of Christ.

Earlier mentioned in chapter four; the church of Jesus Christ is already delving in a dispensation in which believers will no more relationship with God based on denomination and power demonstration, but on the knowledge of Christ Jesus.
*'Whom we are preaching, guiding and teaching every man in all wisdom, so that every man may be complete in Christ Jesus.'***(Col 1:28)**

Branding of vision has taken over denominations so much that everyone now focuses on what their followers desire, living out the Essence; bringing the people to a measure that can make them complete in Christ Jesus.

Stature is the Greek word "hēlikia" which means maturity or adult age.

Biblically, stature is the position or rank you occupy as a result of your knowledge and understanding of Jesus Christ as the son of God. The knowledge of Christ determines your ranking or position both in the physical and in the spiritual realm.

As the physical body needs afoot to develop and grow healthier, so too then spirit man in us needs spiritual nutrients.

For you to get to an adult age in the spirit, there is a need to fill the vacuum in the spirit by the knowledge of Christ which can vivify our spirit man in us. The stature of every Christian is measured only in the word of God which is the standard and of which all things consist.

'He made all things, and without him was not anything made that was made.'
(John 1:3)
'That the God of our Lord Jesus Christ, the Father of glory, may give unto you the spirit of wisdom and revelation in the knowledge of him.'
(Eph 1:17)

The scripture says that they might grow in the spiritual wisdom and knowledge of the son of God.

It's very important to know that, the knowledge of the son of God, gives you a stature; which is the reward of the saints. Every believer has been called to that state of perfection which is the mature age; our generation is fortunate to have been in the dispensation of the revelation of Christ, which many people in the Old Testament saw but could not live Him and the Angels desired but did not have. Jesus was born in the law of Moses but we live it. When the time came for him to reveal His mission and purpose, no one paid attention to Him according to the prophecy.

'Therefore speak I to them in parables: because they seeing see not; and hearing they hear not, neither do they understand.'
(Mat 13:13)

So you can see that even though they were with Jesus, they were not partakers of this gift of God. See what Jesus said to the disciples;

'Henceforth I call you not servants; for the servant knoweth not what his lord doeth: but I have called you friends; for all things that I have heard of my Father I have made known unto you.'
(John 15:15)

'And he said unto them, Unto you it is given to know the mystery of the kingdom of God: but unto them that are without, all these things are done in parables.'
(Mar 4:11)

It has pleased God to reveal the mystery of His kingdom to them that are ready to sit and study the word of God that will bring you to the place of the measure of the stature; maturity in the will of God and to enhance the unity of faith.

CHAPTER EIGHT

THE FULLNESS OF CHRIST

«If you want to attain your God-given aspiration and ambition turn your ears to God's voice »

For in him dwelleth all the fulness of the Godhead bodily.

Col 2:9

The word Fullness means complete, which is to say the entirety of something or to fill to the top so that nothing shall be needed again. But in this perspective, it explains the Godhead as the person of Jesus Christ.

'Blessed be the God and Father of our Lord Jesus Christ, who hath blessed us with all spiritual blessings in heavenly places in Christ.'
(Eph 1:3)
Each time there is a problem of character in a society or in leading the community or group, there are bound to be inevitable jealousy, striving, hatred and disunity.

Till today, the world is suffering from the syndrome of character in all workers of life, this dromedary has become the lifestyle that is exhibited in Christianity, and we can see the rippling effects of such ungodly manner in our societies daily.

> The reason why in verse 11- 12 the apostle Paul makes mention of some spiritual gifts like, Apostle, prophet, evangelist, and teacher, which he was one of them. He clearly stated the reasons for these gifts

> 'And he gave some, apostles; and some, prophets; and some, evangelists; and some, pastors and teachers; For the perfecting of the saints, for the work of the ministry, for the edifying of the body of Christ'

(Eph 4:11-12)

1. Was equip (perfecting) of the saints
2. Work of ministry
3. Building up the body of Christ.
   Now, why did Apostle Paul name only five gifts?
   Note this that when the head (leader) is being attacked all others successfully under his care will easily be trapped down.
   Targeting they who are supposed to be emulated by the faithful in breeding up schism, God's desired purpose cannot be attained.

They need direction to be stable in their calling and not to be derailed from their God-given purpose and the principles of leadership according to the standard of God.

This was a rebuke from God's servant so they can attain their God called purpose; which was preaching the resurrected Jesus Christ.

'And he said unto me, these sayings are faithful and true: and the Lord God of the holy prophets sent his angel to show unto his servants the things which must shortly be done. Behold, I come quickly: blessed is he that kept the sayings of the prophecy of this book. And I John saw these things and heard them. And when I had heard and seen, I fell to worship before the feet of the angel which showed me these things.' **(Rev 22:6-8(KJV)**

God is always watching over us so we should not go astray. That is why he will always send a message to first warn us in our ministerial life as a Christian. Then before he does something, he makes sure to reveal it to his children as in the above mention. If you want to attain your God-given aspiration and ambition turn your ears to God's voice

Amos 3:7;

'Surely the Lord GOD will do nothing, but he revealed his secret unto his servants the prophets.'

Heb 3:15;

'While it is said, Today if ye will hear his voice, harden not your hearts, as in the provocation.'

APPRAISAL

The Supreme Mission of Christ; who is Head of the CHURCH, into the world was the Redemption of man by a life of Perfect Obedience, culminating in offering Himself once and for all. This constituted a full, perfect and sufficient sacrifice for a perfect Ministry of Reconciliation which was foreordained for all believers who are – the CHURCH; His earthly body.

This mission of Christ sets the platform for the Church to operate on. The purpose of Redeeming humanity as Jesus practiced should be lead in the mission of the Church. Soul profiting should be the main benefit for the functioning of the Church.

More so, to achieve this and let the fulfillment of the purpose of the Church be fulfilled, the greasing prerequisite for achieving was just Obedience to the will of the Supreme Head of the Church – Christ.

Obedience to His will helps to build a stress-free and unstrained Church. Obedience exposes and activates His authority over the Church. This is the greatest handicap of the 20th century Church; looking at the total passing on to God as a subsidiary. God is used as the second option to address ministerial strides towards achieving its Redemptive Purpose.

Our portion of write up brings a clarion call awakener to the hour of decision and destiny of the Church. Its either we move on with God or settle for what we are currently enjoying; the safety of the Institutional and Traditional structures we operate today as the Church.

Meanwhile, *the Church still strives to the end of Entering into His Rest Atlast. There is a need to go back to the Tenets of the Christian Faith.* These tenets are the fundamental basics of Christianity which must be respected to ensure the Horizontal attachment of the Church its purpose and relevance.

The focus text of this paper begins with this signal, reminder, and prerequisite for the fulfilled relevance of the Church; *"Till we all come"* implying there is yet a process and path to pursue and to arrive at a common ground as a Body of Christ.

Mention must be made to the emphasis of the oneness of vision, purpose, foundation, destiny, and essence of the Church is noted; *"TheUnity of the Faith."* This means that the Christian Faith has a unifying basis and destiny that binds the body of Christ. It must be respected and recognized in its relevance as an identical unified structure with a set and Divine purpose.

The words of Jesus to Peter are the ultimate Declaration of Christ about the establishment of the Church. When Peter declares Jesus as; *'theChrist'* Jesus went on to affirm; *'On this Rock, I will build my Church'*- He was not referring to Peter to be the rock as many put it. The Rock referred to here, was the affirmation by Faith and of Faith that Jesus was the Christ. This tangible affirmation is to be the only platform for Action of the Church.

If all these are respected and implored, then the Spiritual Audacity and status quo of the CHURCH will be re-enacted, and purpose will be achieved most of all with a united unified body.

The Alloyed Church

BIBLIOGRAPHY

Gene, A. Getz, The Walk. Broadman & Holman Publishers, USA.
John, Byler,. Sign Posts for the Journey. LeaderServe Publishers, USA.
Roger, Bowen,. So I Send You. Ashford Colour Press. London.
Allen, R,. Ministry of the Spirit. Eerdmans, Grand Rapids.
Anderson, W,. The Church in East Africa 1840-1976. CTP, Dodoma, Tanzania.
Dr.Bernard, Etta,. Demystifying Purpose, USA
Barrett, D,. Schism and Renewal in Africa. Oxford University Press, Oxford.
Finney, J., Church on the Move. Daybreak(DLT), London.
Dr.Bernard, Etta., Class Journals\Notes, Douala, Cameroon.
Donovan, V., Christianity Rediscovered. SCM Press, London.
Dr.Bernard, Etta., Understanding bliblical chemistrytUSA.
Mike, Murdock., The Assignment. Albury Publishing, USA.
William, M. Branham., Why I'm Against Organised Religion. Voice of God Recordings, USA.
T. L., Osborn., How to have the Good Life. Osborn Foundation, USA.
Robert, K. Greenleaf, Servant Leadership. Paulist Press, USA.

The Alloyed Church

NOTES

The Missing link in Contemporary Christianity

Made in the USA
Columbia, SC
29 October 2018